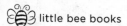 little bee books

An imprint of Bonnier Publishing USA
251 Park Avenue South, New York, NY 10010
Copyright © 2018 by Bonnier Publishing USA
All rights reserved, including the right of reproduction in whole or in part in any form.
Little Bee Books is a trademark of Bonnier Publishing USA, and associated colophon is a trademark of Bonnier Publishing USA.
Manufactured in China TPL 0418
ISBN 978-1-4998-0621-2 (hc)
First Edition 10 9 8 7 6 5 4 3 2 1
ISBN 978-1-4998-0620-5 (pbk)
First Edition 10 9 8 7 6 5 4 3 2 1

Library of Congress Cataloging-in-Publication Data
Names: Ohlin, Nancy, author. | Simó, Roger, illustrator.
Title: Pearl Harbor / by Nancy Ohlin; illustrated by Roger Simó.
Description: First edition. | New York, New York: Little Bee Books, 2018.
Series: Blast back! | Includes bibliographical references.
Audience: Age 7–10. | Audience: Grade 4 to 6. | Identifiers: LCCN 2017055704
Subjects: LCSH: Pearl Harbor (Hawaii), Attack on, 1941—Juvenile literature.
Classification: LCC D767.92 .O35 2018 | DDC 940.54/26693—dc23
LC record available at https://lccn.loc.gov/2017055704

littlebeebooks.com
bonnierpublishingusa.com

BLAST BACK!

PEARL HARBOR

by Nancy Ohlin   **illustrated by Roger Simó**

little bee books

CONTENTS

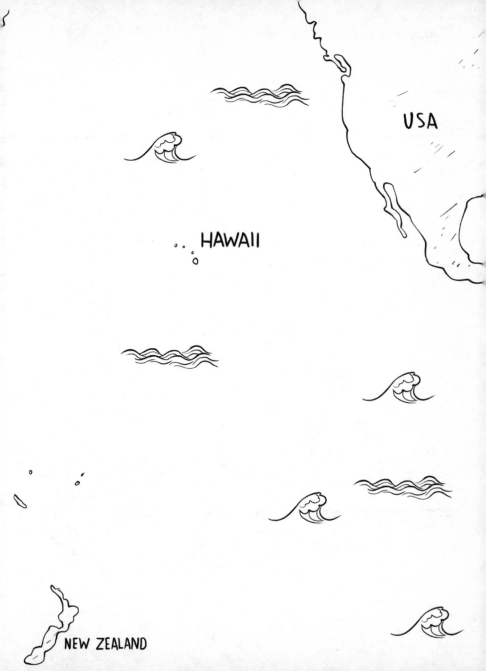

Introduction

Have you ever heard people mention Pearl Harbor and wondered what they were talking about? Where is Pearl Harbor? What happened there, and why was it important historically?

Let's blast back in time for a little adventure and find out. . . .

PEARL HARBOR

11

A Brief History of Pearl Harbor

Pearl Harbor is a harbor in Hawaii. A harbor is a place along a coastline where ships and other vessels can safely dock. Hawaii is made up of more than a hundred islands, including eight main islands, seven of which are inhabited.

The United States Navy has a base at Pearl Harbor. It has been there since 1899, sixty years before Hawaii became an American state in 1959.

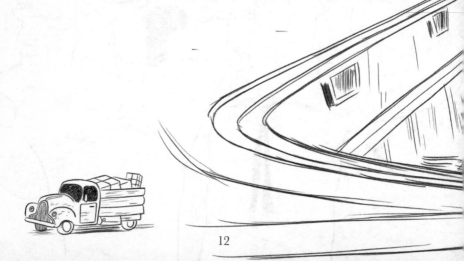

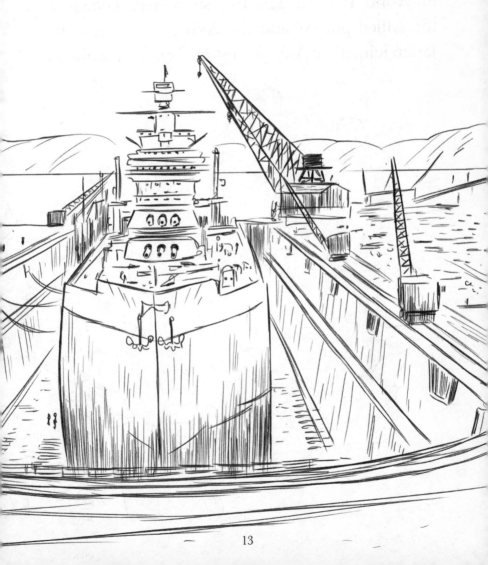

Starting in 1939, much of the world was engaged in World War II. The two sides were known as the Allied powers and the Axis powers. In 1940, Japan joined the Axis powers by forming a military

alliance with Germany, Italy, and other countries. At that time, the major Allied powers consisted of Great Britain, France, the Soviet Union, and China—but not the United States.

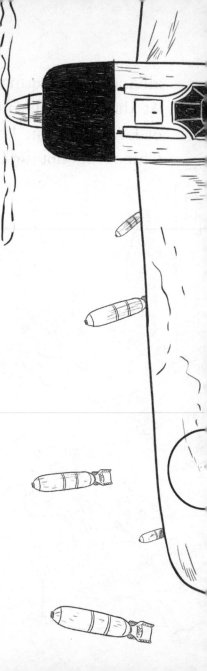

On December 7, 1941, Japanese warplanes carried out a surprise aerial attack on the Pearl Harbor naval base, even though the US had not officially entered the war. The attack followed a decade of tensions between Japan and the US.

Over 2,300 Americans died in the attack. On December 8, the US joined the Allied powers and declared war against Japan and the other Axis powers.

The term "Pearl Harbor" can refer to the December 7 attack, the naval base, or the harbor.

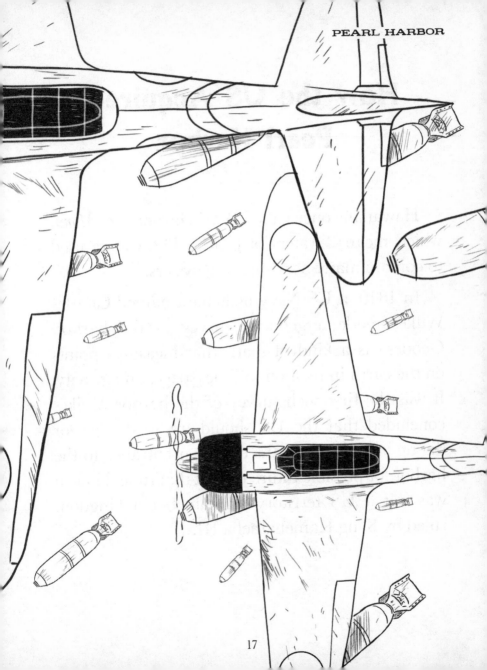

How the US Acquired Pearl Harbor

Hawaiians once called Pearl Harbor *Wai Momi*, which means "waters of pearl." The waters used to contain many pearl-bearing oysters.

In 1840, a US Navy lieutenant named Charles Wilkes made a geodetic survey of the harbor. Geodesy is a kind of math that measures points on the earth in relation to time, space, and gravity. It was the first such survey of the harbor. Wilkes concluded that the US should try to dredge (or dig up and clear out) the coral-bar entrance to the harbor for possible future use. At that time, Hawaii was not a US territory or state but a kingdom ruled by King Kamehameha III.

PEARL HARBOR

In 1873, an American military officer named John McAllister Schofield was given an assignment by the secretary of war, William Belknap, to determine if the US should set up a military presence in Hawaii. After consideration, Schofield recommended that the US try to create a military base in Pearl Harbor because of its strategic location in the Pacific.

But the US didn't actually have the right to create a base there—or even to dredge it, as Wilkes had suggested three decades earlier. All this changed when the US entered the Reciprocity Treaty of 1875 with Hawaii. This free-trade agreement allowed the two governments to give each other special treatment. When the treaty was renewed in 1887, it included a new condition that allowed the US exclusive rights to build a naval base at Pearl Harbor.

Hawaii's Beginnings

Hawaii's first settlers likely came from the Marquesas Islands in the South Pacific Ocean, possibly in the fourth or fifth century, and a second wave of settlers came from Tahiti, possibly in the ninth or tenth century.

For many centuries, Hawaii existed in relative isolation from the rest of the world. Then, in January of 1778, Captain James Cook and his British fleet arrived on Hawaiian shores.

After their arrival, Hawaii was no longer an isolated place. Americans and Europeans sailed to Hawaii to see if there might be trade to conduct, natural resources to tap, or land to colonize. Missionaries came to try to convert the Hawaiians to Christianity. The influx of foreigners diluted and forever altered ancient Hawaiian customs, traditions, and beliefs. Political power also shifted as the foreigners, especially Americans, settled in Hawaii and sought to enhance and preserve their business and economic interests there.

The American Annexation of Hawaii

Until 1810, Hawaii was made up of different kingdoms that were ruled by local chiefs. After 1810, Hawaii was ruled as one kingdom, first by King Kamehameha I and, later, by his descendants as well as two monarchs from the Kalakaua dynasty. The last monarch was Queen Liliuokalani, who ruled until 1893, when she was forced to step down from her throne to pave the way for the American annexation, or takeover, of the islands.

Why did the Americans want to annex Hawaii? After all, they already had the rights to build a naval base at Pearl Harbor because of the Reciprocity Treaty.

Americans were interested in Hawaii for many reasons besides building a naval base. One of those reasons was sugar. The American Civil War (which lasted from 1861 to 1865) had made the price of US-produced sugar skyrocket. Hawaii had plentiful sugar plantations, and Americans wanted to buy sugar from them—and invest in them too. In fact, after the Reciprocity Treaty of 1875, American sugar plantation owners came to Hawaii and bought up many plantations so they could export and sell sugar to Americans back home.

These American plantation owners in Hawaii became more and more vested in Hawaiian politics and laws and in protecting their own business interests. In 1893, they helped force Queen Liliuokalani to step down from the throne and replace her with temporary leaders with strong ties to the US.

Five years later, the Spanish-American War broke out, and the US sent troops to Spanish-occupied Cuba to aid a local rebellion against Spain. The US won quickly and easily because of its superior military. As a result of the war, the US gained new colonies in Latin America (Guam and Puerto Rico) and the Pacific (the Philippines).

Now the US had an even stronger stake in the Pacific; they had a colony to govern and protect there. The new US president, William McKinley, approved the annexation of Hawaii in 1898, and Hawaii became an American territory.

The Building of the Naval Base

The US began building the naval base at Pearl Harbor in the early 1900s. When it was completed, it became the naval base for the US Pacific Fleet (USPACFLT). To this day, this fleet provides naval forces to the United States Pacific Command, which is responsible for military operations in the Indo-Asia-Pacific region, an area spanning more than 100 million square miles.

The Pearl Harbor naval base covers an area that is equivalent to 10,000 acres, including ten square miles of water that can be sailed (aka "navigable water") and hundreds of spots for ships and boats to anchor in (aka "anchorages"). A channel called the Pearl Harbor Entrance connects the harbor to the Pacific Ocean.

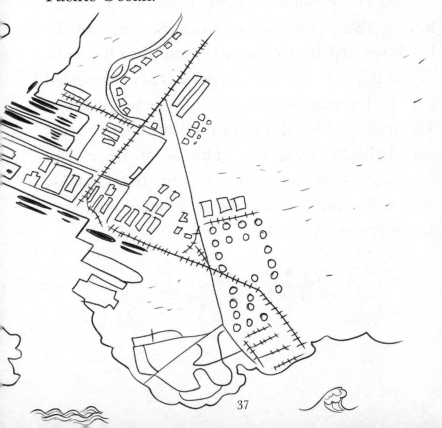

37

The US and Japan Before Pearl Harbor

Like Hawaii, Japan had been isolated from the rest of the world for many centuries. Then, on July 8, 1853, Commodore Matthew Perry of the US Navy and his troops sailed into Edo Bay (now Tokyo Bay) in a fleet of warships. They demanded that the Japanese people enter a treaty with the US. The treaty, which favored American interests, was signed the following year. This began decades of Americans and Europeans forcing the Japanese into trade and diplomatic relations that were advantageous to the West.

The Japanese government grew to believe that the only way to get its power and autonomy back was to achieve equality with the West. To this end, it began to try to expand its territory in the Pacific. It became embroiled in an extended conflict with China over land, including a war from 1894 to 1895 over who controlled Korea. From 1904 to 1905, Japan also fought a war against Russia over Korea and Manchuria, in China. In 1931, Japan invaded

Manchuria, which resulted in a second war between Japan and China that lasted until the end of World War II in 1945.

The US did not approve of what Japan was doing to China and began imposing sanctions on Japan. These sanctions included limiting the import of American oil, steel, and other supplies, which Japan needed for its war effort. The sanctions increased tensions between Japan and the US.

Japanese Immigration to America

Starting in the late-nineteenth century, many Japanese citizens took advantage of the end of their country's isolation. Between 1886 and 1911, hundreds of thousands of Japanese citizens immigrated to the US in search of prosperity. New laws in the US that restricted Chinese immigrants made Americans eager to recruit Japanese immigrants for labor, especially for building railroads.

As with other immigrants from Europe and elsewhere, though, the Japanese faced difficult adjustments, harsh working conditions, racism, and prejudice.

World War II Begins

On the other side of the globe, World War II began in Europe in September of 1939 when Nazi Germany invaded Poland. Between 1939 and 1945, the war grew to involve three main theaters, or areas of conflict: the European theater, the Pacific theater, and the North African theater.

Japan decided to join the Axis powers in 1940, in part because it needed the support of Germany and the other countries to continue its expansion into the Pacific. This alliance was also a way to send a warning to the US not to enter the war on the side of the Allied powers.

Until the end of 1941, the US maintained an isolationist position regarding the war, although they sent military aid to Great Britain and other Allied powers. American citizens were against entering the war over problems that were happening in faraway places.

San Francisco Chronicle

NAZIS TAKE PARIS!

Desperate Negotiations

In July of 1941, Japan succeeded in occupying Indochina and was poised to continue occupying other lands throughout the region such as Malaya and the oil-rich Dutch East Indies. The US government responded with more and harsher sanctions. It froze Japanese assets, such as money and property, in America and it completely stopped, or embargoed, the shipment of oil to Japan.

This was followed by months of negotiations between Japan and the US. The US insisted that Japan give up all its newly acquired territories in exchange for the lifting of sanctions and other considerations. But Japan refused, and the two sides were at a dangerous stalemate as the specter of war hovered over the two countries.

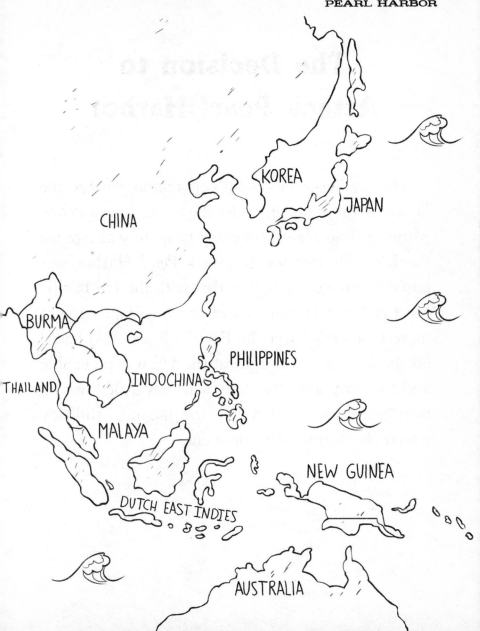

The Decision to Attack Pearl Harbor

During the unsuccessful negotiation process, the Japanese government, under the leadership of Prime Minister Tojo Hideki, decided to go to war against the US. The decision to attack Pearl Harbor was based partly on the notion that with the US Pacific Fleet at Pearl Harbor out of the way, Japan might more easily take over the Pacific. It was also based on the idea that war against the US was inevitable and that crippling the American naval fleet would demonstrate to the US that the Japanese military would be a formidable opponent.

However, Japan didn't officially declare war on the US or send a list of ultimatums (such as "you must meet our demands or we will attack") before striking. On November 26, 1941, a Japanese fleet including six aircraft carriers, eleven destroyers, three cruisers, and two battleships sailed to a spot about 275 miles north of Hawaii. Their leader was Vice Admiral Nagumo Chuichi. From there, 360 Japanese planes were launched. They maintained absolute

radio silence—that is, they didn't communicate to one another over radio waves—so they could ensure surprise and secrecy.

The goal once they reached the Pearl Harbor naval base was to destroy the ships on "Battleship Row" as well as the planes on the ground at the Naval Air Station and nearby Wheeler Field and Hickam Field.

54

Can One Country Attack Another When They're Not at War?

The short answer is no. According to the international laws of war first outlined during the Hague Convention of 1907, a country can only attack another country when the two countries are at war or if Country A has to defend itself or another country against Country B's attack. The Hague Conventions were international meetings that set up rules for war—chiefly to prevent unnecessary suffering.

A Sneak Attack?

Did the US know in advance that Japan planned to attack Pearl Harbor?

A top secret twenty-six-page memo from the US Office of Naval Intelligence, dated three days before the Pearl Harbor attack, described a possible Japanese assault on Hawaii. The memo said: "In anticipation of possible open conflict with this country, Japan is vigorously utilizing every available agency to secure military, naval, and commercial information, paying particular attention to the West Coast, the Panama Canal, and the Territory of Hawaii." The memo also flagged Japan's surveillance of Hawaii under a section called "Methods of Operation and Points of Attack."

The memo suggests that the US was aware Japan was considering an attack on Hawaii, although the exact details—such as when, how, and the exact target—were not known.

The Message That Didn't Make It in Time

Before the Pearl Harbor attack, the Japanese government sent a message to the US, officially breaking off diplomatic relations. This meant that Japan was no longer going to try to resolve its differences with the US. That message was supposed to reach the US secretary of state before the Pearl Harbor attack. But due to problems with decoding and translation, the message didn't reach the secretary of state until after the attack. Had it received the message in time, the US government might have realized that war between the two countries was imminent.

December 7, 1941

Around 7:55 a.m. Hawaii time on December 7, which was around 1:55 p.m. in Washington, D.C., and around 2:55 a.m. the next day in Japan, nearly two hundred Japanese bombers, fighters, torpedo planes, and other aircraft appeared over the Pearl Harbor naval base and began dropping bombs and torpedoes. Because it was a Sunday morning, many of the 780 American antiaircraft guns were unmanned. (The purpose of antiaircraft guns is to protect against enemy planes and other aircraft.) Many of the soldiers were asleep in their beds; others were on shore leave, or mini vacations, for the weekend.

Radar at the naval base had detected the incoming planes before the attack. But the officers on duty had mistaken them for American B-17 military planes arriving from the West Coast.

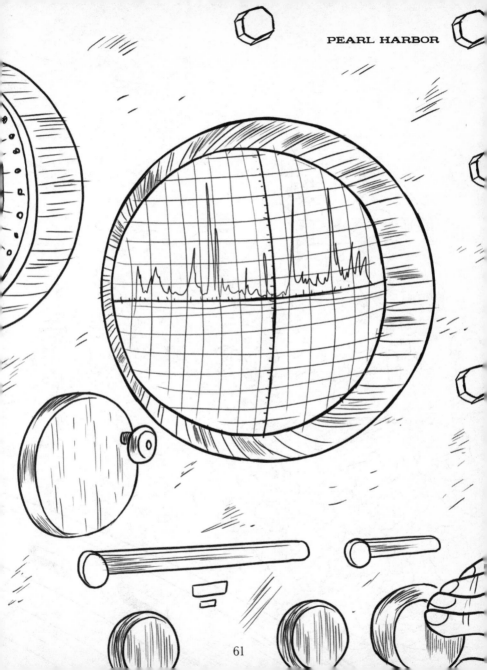

BLAST BACK!

About an hour later, a second wave of 168 Japanese planes arrived and began bombing. By the end of the attack, over 2,300 US military personnel had died, and another 1,100 or so had been wounded. More than 180 aircraft were destroyed, as was the battleship *Arizona*. The battleship *Oklahoma* capsized (or turned over), and three other battleships, the *West Virginia*, *Nevada*, and *California*, sank. There was damage to many other vessels too, including

three destroyers, three cruisers, and three additional battleships.

The Japanese losses were far less: an estimated one or two fleet submarines, five midget submarines, somewhere between twenty-nine and sixty planes, and fewer than one hundred troops.

Later that same day, Japan officially declared war on the US and the British Empire.

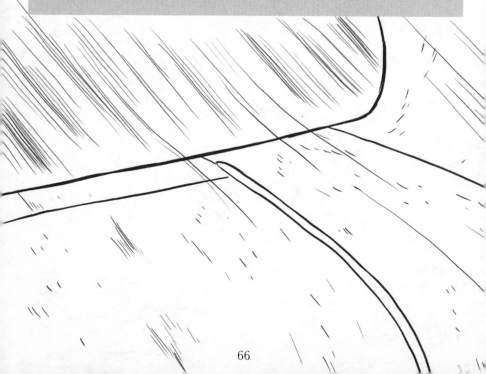

Tora, Tora, Tora

The radio message "tora, tora, tora" was conveyed by a Japanese fighter after the first wave of planes attacked Pearl Harbor to confirm the planes had accomplished their mission. The word *tora* means "tiger" in Japanese. But in this instance, it was a code phrase that meant "lightning attack."

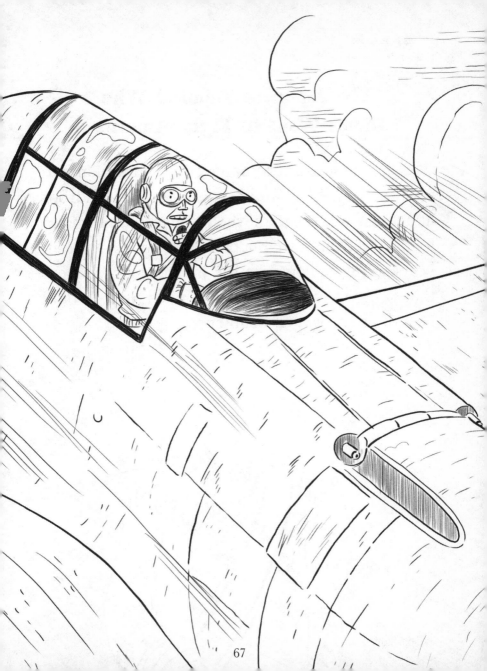

The Japanese Admiral Who Didn't Want to Fight America

A Japanese admiral named Isoroku Yamamoto was known as the "architect" of the Pearl Harbor attack. He was the man who came up with the plan for an aerial ambush. But before the attack, he spent years trying to convince the Japanese government that going to war against the United States would be a disaster for their country.

Yamamoto graduated from the Japanese Naval Academy in 1904. During his naval career, he traveled throughout Europe and the US and studied at Harvard for two years. From 1926 to 1928, he had a diplomatic post in Washington, D.C. He read English-language books and newspapers, and he admired President Abraham Lincoln as a "champion" of "human freedom."

As Yamamoto climbed the ranks to become commander in chief of the Japanese Combined Fleet in the late 1930s, he tried to keep Japan from forming an alliance with Nazi Germany. But the government ignored his advice.

Yamamoto knew that Japan didn't have the strength or supplies to carry on a long-term war against the US, saying: "We must not start a war with so little chance of success." He suggested that they pull out of their alliance with Germany and Italy and pull troops out of China. But none of this happened, and Yamamoto knew his cause was lost. He supported a surprise aerial attack that he hoped would disable the US Navy in the Pacific and force the United States into a negotiated peace and avoid war. This plan was set in motion on December 7 when Japanese warplanes attacked Pearl Harbor.

The US Reaction

On the afternoon of December 7, President Franklin D. Roosevelt received a phone call from his secretary of war, Henry Stimson, telling him about the Pearl Harbor attack. President Roosevelt met with his military advisers, and around 5:00 p.m., he drafted a request to Congress—the lawmaking body of the federal government—asking for a declaration of war against Japan.

Before December 7, Americans had been reluctant to get involved in a world war that was happening "far away." The devastating attack on Pearl Harbor changed the public sentiment since it had happened on American soil. Now the US was willing to enter the fray.

On December 8 at 12:30 p.m., President Roosevelt read his request for a declaration of war in a joint session of Congress. His speech was broadcast on the radio to the nation. Congress voted almost unanimously in favor of war. The only congressperson to vote no against a declaration of war on Japan was Congresswoman Jeannette Rankin from Montana, who in 1916 had become the first woman to be elected to Congress. She was a pacifist and opposed war and violence.

At four o'clock, President Roosevelt signed the declaration. (By then, Great Britain had already declared war against Japan.)

Three days later, on December 11, Germany and Italy declared war on the US, and in response, the US declared war on Germany and Italy. Now the US was embroiled in two theaters of war: Europe and the Pacific.

"A Date Which Will Live in Infamy"

President Roosevelt's speech to Congress and the nation began:

Yesterday, December 7, 1941—a date which will live in infamy—the United States of America was suddenly and deliberately attacked by naval and air forces of the Empire of Japan.

The United States was at the moment at peace with that nation and, at the solicitation of Japan, was still in conversation with its government and its emperor looking toward the maintenance of peace in the Pacific.

BLAST BACK!

He went on to explain that on the evening of December 7 and the morning of December 8, Japan had proceeded to attack Hong Kong, Guam, the Philippine Islands, Wake Island, and Midway Island, all in the Pacific.

I ask that the Congress declare that since the unprovoked and dastardly attack by Japan on Sunday, December 7, a state of war has existed between the United States and the Japanese Empire.

USS *Arizona* Leaks Fuel to This Day

On December 6, 1941, the USS *Arizona* got a full tank of fuel (around 1.5 million gallons!) in preparation for a trip to the mainland scheduled for later in the month. After the attack, the USS *Arizona* burned for two days, but still 2–9 quarts of fuel leak from the wreckage each day and bubble up to the surface of the water. The National Park Service has been researching the leak since 1998 to better understand the rate of deterioration of the USS *Arizona* and how it may affect its surrounding environment.

The Japanese American Detention Camps

On December 18, 1941, President Roosevelt signed the War Powers Act, an emergency law that increased the powers of the executive branch of the government during the war. In March of 1942, he signed a second War Powers Act that further increased those powers.

These increased powers paved the way for President Roosevelt to issue Executive Order 9066 on February 19, 1942. This order authorized the secretary of war and other military leaders to assign certain portions of the US as "military areas" and remove its residents, with the help of troops if necessary, for the purposes of "national security." These areas happened to be where many people of Japanese descent lived and worked.

This executive order resulted in the forcible removal of nearly 120,000 Japanese Americans, including children, from their homes in California and other western states. They were incarcerated, or held, in one of ten detention camps, all with barbed-wire fences and armed guards. Most of these people were US citizens or had legal, permanent status to live in the country.

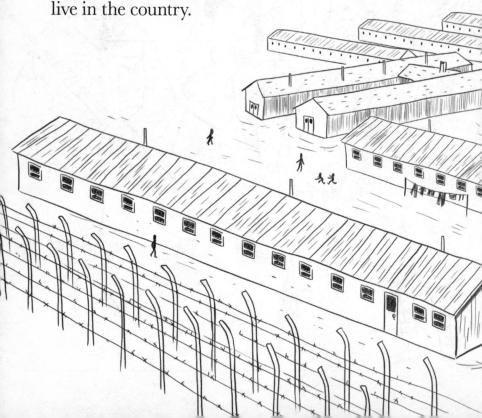

President Roosevelt claimed that these relocations and incarcerations were necessary to prevent espionage (or spying) and sabotage by the Japanese Americans, and to "protect" them from Americans who now mistrusted and feared them.

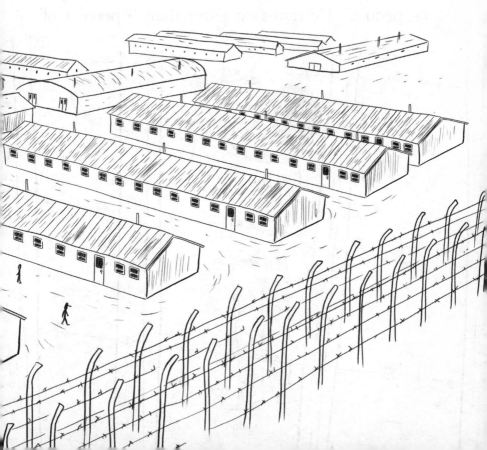

The roundups of the Japanese Americans had begun within forty-eight hours after the Pearl Harbor attack. In January 1942, a naval intelligence officer in Los Angeles questioned the roundups, observing that Japanese Americans were being targeted almost entirely "because of the physical characteristics of the people." He said that fewer than 3 percent of

them might be potential spies and saboteurs. But the government ignored his statement and continued to cast the widest net possible. John DeWitt, the army general in charge of the West Coast, insensitively said at the time: "A Jap's a Jap. They are a dangerous element, whether loyal or not."

The 442nd Regimental Combat Team

While the US was at war with Japan and incarcerating many of its Japanese Americans in detention camps, a combat unit of Japanese Americans was fighting on the side of the US. The 442nd Regimental Combat Team had been assembled by the US government to fight in Europe. By the end of the war, more than 13,000 of them had served in the war for their country, and more than 700 had been killed or were missing in action. They became famous as the most highly decorated unit of its size in US military history.

In addition to the members of the 442nd, an additional 6,000 or so Japanese Americans served in the Military Intelligence Service and helped decipher and translate important Japanese codes and documents.

The Dropping of
the Atomic Bombs

By the spring of 1945, the Allied powers had nearly won the war in Europe and North Africa. But the war in the Pacific raged on. Even though Japan seemed destined to surrender, as Italy had done on September 8, 1943, and Germany had done on May 7, 1945, its troops continued inflicting heavy casualties on Allied troops in the Pacific.

The US had been conducting bombing raids on Japan since soon after the Pearl Harbor attack. A bombing raid of Tokyo in March 1945, nicknamed "Operation Meetinghouse," killed over an estimated 100,000 civilians. The Japanese refer to this event as the "Night of the Black Snow."

General Douglas A. MacArthur and other military leaders wanted to bring about Japan's defeat with more bombing raids and a ground invasion—a strategy nicknamed "Operation Downfall." They informed President Harry S. Truman (who had taken over as president on April 12, 1945, upon President Roosevelt's death) that such a strategy might work but could result in nearly a million US casualties.

President Truman didn't want to risk such a high casualty number. But the war with Japan had to be ended somehow. A decision was made to drop two atomic bombs on two key Japanese cities. On August 6, an American plane called *Enola Gay* dropped an atomic bomb on Hiroshima; three days later, another American plane, *Bockscar*, dropped an atomic bomb on Nagasaki. Well over 100,000 people are believed to have died in the bombings.

The atomic bombs proved to be the final blows. Japan formally surrendered to the US on September 2 on the deck of the US battleship *Missouri*.

The Legacy of Pearl Harbor

After the end of the war, the Allied powers ordered a military occupation of Japan. The occupation was headed by General Douglas MacArthur. Its purpose was to punish, reform, and rebuild Japan. Japan was also stripped of its army. The occupation ended in 1952.

In 1988, US President Ronald Reagan signed
the Civil Liberties Act to formally apologize to the
more than 100,000 Japanese Americans who were
incarcerated during World War II and to compensate
the surviving victims.

During the Korean War (1950–1953) and Vietnam War (1955–1975), troops and equipment were staged and coordinated at Pearl Harbor before being sent off to combat zones. Today, Pearl Harbor continues

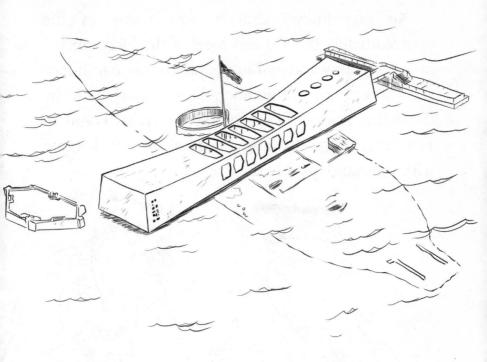

to be an active naval base and headquarters of the US Pacific Fleet. It has also been a National Historic Landmark since 1964 and is visited by almost two million people each year. The site includes many important attractions including a USS *Arizona* memorial that was built directly above where the battleship *Arizona* sank on December 7, 1941.

No one knows exactly how many of the approximately 60,000 survivors of the December 7 attack are alive today. But people continue to honor their service and remember the sacrifice made by the fallen troops. Some of the survivors come to Pearl Harbor on the anniversary of the attack along with thousands of others.

Today, the US and Japan have a strong political and economic relationship that nevertheless acknowledges their difficult history. On May 27, 2016, seventy-one years after the dropping of the atomic bombs, US President Barack Obama visited Hiroshima. There, he gave a speech acknowledging the atrocities of the past, saying: "The world was forever changed here, but today the children of this city will go through their day in peace. What a precious thing that is. It is worth protecting, and then extending to every child. This is a future we can choose, a future in which Hiroshima and Nagasaki are known not as the dawn of atomic warfare but as the beginning of our moral awakening."

Later that year, President Obama and Prime Minister Shinzo Abe of Japan together visited Pearl Harbor following the seventy-fifth anniversary of the December 7 attack. They laid wreaths at the site as Prime Minister Abe offered "sincerest and everlasting condolences" to the victims of the attack, adding: "We must never repeat the horrors of war again. This is the solemn vow that the people of Japan have taken."

Well, it's been a great adventure. Goodbye, Pearl Harbor!

Where to next?

Also available:

ANCIENT EGYPT
by Nancy Ohlin
Illustrated by Adam Larkum

ANCIENT GREECE
by Nancy Ohlin
Illustrated by Adam Larkum

THE GREAT WALL OF CHINA
by Nancy Ohlin
Illustrated by Adam Larkum

VIKINGS
by Nancy Ohlin
Illustrated by Adam Larkum

THE SALEM WITCH TRIALS
by Nancy Ohlin
Illustrated by Roger Simó

THE AMERICAN REVOLUTION
by Nancy Ohlin
Illustrated by Adam Larkum

THE CIVIL WAR
by Nancy Ohlin
Illustrated by Adam Larkum

THE STATUE OF LIBERTY
by Nancy Ohlin
Illustrated by Roger Simó

THE TITANIC
by Nancy Ohlin
Illustrated by Adam Larkum

WORLD WAR II
by Nancy Ohlin
Illustrated by Roger Simó

THE CIVIL RIGHTS MOVEMENT
by Nancy Ohlin
Illustrated by Roger Simó

THE SPACE RACE
by Nancy Ohlin
Illustrated by Roger Simó

Selected Bibliography

"'A Day Which Will Live in Infamy': The First Typed Draft of Franklin D. Roosevelt's War Address." *National Archives*. https://www.archives.gov/education/lessons/day-of-infamy.

"Bombing of Hiroshima and Nagasaki." *History*. http://www.history.com/topics/world-war-ii/bombing-of-hiroshima-and-nagasaki.

Britannica Kids. kids.britannica.com.

Encyclopedia Britannica. www.britannica.com.

Goddard, Jacqui. "Pearl Harbour Memo Shows US Warned of Japanese Attack." *Telegraph*. December 4, 2011. http://www.telegraph.co.uk/news/worldnews/northamerica/usa/8932197/Pearl-Harbour-memo-shows-US-warned-of-Japanese-attack.html.

Maranzani, Barbara. "Unlikely World War II Soldiers Awarded Nation's Highest Honor." *History*. November 3, 2011. http://www.history.com/news/unlikely-world-war-ii-soldiers-awarded-nations-highest-honor.

McManus, Malia Mattoch. "Elderly Survivors Commemorate Pearl Harbor Attack." *Reuters*. December 7, 2013. http://www.reuters.com/article/us-usa-pearlharbor-idUSBRE9B606620131208.

"The Path to Pearl Harbor." *National World War II Museum*. https://www.nationalww2museum.org/war/articles/path-pearl-harbor.

Qureshi, Bilal. "From Wrong to Right: A US Apology for Japanese Internment." *NPR*. August 9, 2013. http://www.npr.org/sections/codeswitch/2013/08/09/210138278/japanese-internment-redress.

"Text of President Obama's Speech in Hiroshima, Japan." *New York Times*. May 27, 2016. https://www.nytimes.com/2016/05/28/world/asia/text-of-president-obamas-speech-in-hiroshima-japan.html.

Toll, Ian W. "A Reluctant Enemy." *New York Times*. December 6, 2011. http://www.nytimes.com/2011/12/07/opinion/a-reluctant-enemy.html.

NANCY OHLIN is the author of the YA novels *Always, Forever* and *Beauty* as well as the early chapter book series Greetings from Somewhere under the pseudonym Harper Paris. She lives in Ithaca, New York, with her husband, their two kids, four cats, and assorted animals who happen to show up at their door. Visit her online at nancyohlin.com.

ROGER SIMÓ is an illustrator based in a town near Barcelona, where he lives with his wife, son, and daughter. He has become the person that he would have envied when he was a child: someone who makes a living by drawing and explaining fantastic stories.